PRAY &

Pause

An interactive Prayer Journal to
cultivate your conversations with God.

MARCIE Y. LEGGETT

Copyright© 2024 by Marcie Y. Leggett
Pray & Pause
First edition May 2024

All rights reserved. No part of this book may be reproduced in any form by any electronic or mechanical means, including photocopying, recording, or information storage and retrieval without permission in writing from the author, except in the case of brief quotations embodied in critical articles or reviews. For permission requests, write to the author, addressed "Attention: Permissions Coordinator," at prayandpause@gmail.com.

All scripture quotations, unless otherwise indicated, are taken from the King James Version of the bible.

Scriptures marked KJV are taken from the KING JAMES VERSION (KJV): KING JAMES VERSION, public domain. Scriptures marked AMP are taken from the AMPLIFIED BIBLE (AMP): Scripture taken from the AMPLIFIED BIBLE, Copyright © 1954, 1958, 1962, 1964, 1965, 1987, by the Lockman Foundation. Used by permission. (www.Lockman.org). Scripture quotations taken from the Amplified ® Bible (AMPC), Copyright © 1954, 1958, 1962, 1964, 1965, 1987, by the Lockman Foundation. Used by permission. (www.Lockman.org). Scriptures marked NLT are taken from the HOLY BIBLE, NEW LIVING TRANSLATION (NLT): Scriptures taken from the HOLY BIBLE, NEW LIVING TRANSLATION, Copyright © 1996, 2004, 2007 by Tyndale House Foundation. Scripture quotations marked (NIV) are taken from the HOLY BIBLE, NEW INTERNATIONAL VERSION®, NIV®. Copyright © 1973, 1978, 1984, 2011 by Biblica, Inc.® Used by permission of Zondervan. All rights reserved worldwide. www.zondervan.com The "NIV" and "New International Version" are trademarks registered in the United States Patent and Trademark Office by Biblica, Inc.® Scriptures marked ESV are taken from the HOLY BIBLE ENGLISH STANDARD VERSION (ESV): Scriptures taken from the HOLY BIBLE ENGLISH STANDARD VERSION© Copyright© 2001 by Crossway, a publishing ministry of Good News Publishers. Used by permission. Scripture quotations marked TPT are from The Passion Translation © Copyright © 2017, 2018 by Passion & Fire Ministries, Inc. Used by permission. All rights reserved. ThePassionTranslation.com. Scriptures marked TEV are taken from the TODAY'S ENGLISH VERSION (TEV): Scripture taken from TODAY'S ENGLISH VERSION first edition Copyright © 1976 American Bible Society. Used by permission. Scripture quotations marked MSG are taken from THE MESSAGE, copyright © 1993, 2002, 2018 by Eugene H. Peterson. Used by permission of NavPress. All rights reserved. Represented by Tyndale House Publishers, Inc. Scripture quotations taken from the New American Standard Bible® (NASB), Copyright © 1960, 1962, 1963, 1968, 1971, 1972, 1973, 1975, 1977, 1995 by The Lockman Foundation. Used by permission. www.Lockman.org. CEB scripture references to the Common English Bible (CEB), Copyright © 2011, all rights reserved, are used by permission. Scripture taken from the New King James Version® Copyright © 1982 by Thomas Nelson. Used by permission. All rights reserved. Scripture taken from the New Century Version®. Copyright © 2005 by Thomas Nelson. Used by permission. All rights reserved. Scripture quotations marked TLB are taken from The Living Bible copyright © 1971. Used by permission of Tyndale House Publishers, a Division of Tyndale House Ministries, Carol Stream, Illinois 60188. All rights reserved. Scripture taken from The Modern English Version (MEV) Copyright © 2014 by Military Bible Association. Used by permission. All rights reserved. GOD'S WORD®, © 1995 God's Word to the Nations. Used by permission of God's Word Mission Society.

A few select verses are author paraphrased.

Editor of May 2024 edition: Jordan C. Spruel
Interior design: Marcie Y. Leggett
Cover design: Marcie Y. Leggett
Back cover photograph: Anaya Photography, Baltimore, MD
Raw image attributions: See page 86

ISBN:
Printed in the United States of America

♥

For my sons Marquis, DeShae, and Christian,
and my Grand Littles Sincere, Marli, Cassidy, Mars & Harmony.
My legacy, my inspiration, and the absolute joys of my life.
I love each of you more than you'll ever know.
May the Lord bless you and protect you.
May the Lord smile on you and be gracious to you.
May the Lord show you His favor and give you His peace.

♥

For Mommy (Carolyn), I love you…
Years of watching you daily journal your days
and fall on your knees before God has marked my life.
You are indeed my 'muse' and I'm giving you your flowers.

Foreword
by Portia Taylor

Introducing Marcie Leggett, a bonified prayer solutionist, whose expertise lies in simplifying conversations with God to bring about life-transforming results. As her Pastor, I've had a front row seat to her emphasis on prayer and pausing in the mist of chaos and challenges. She embodies the timeless wisdom found in the scripture that exhorts us to "pray without ceasing" (1 Thessalonians 5:17). Through her steadfast commitment to prayer and unwavering faith, she exemplifies what it means to persevere and not grow weary in seeking God's presence and guidance.

In this book, "Pray and Pause," Marcie offers invaluable insights and guidance on developing a meaningful prayer life. As someone who eliminates every excuse for not engaging in prayer, she empowers readers to embrace the power of pausing to hear from God. Delivering a unique perspective to the importance of prayer and pausing in our fast-paced world, she emphasizes the value of cultivating a deep devotional life with God. This sentiment resonates deeply in today's world, where mental health challenges are prevalent, and the need for inner peace and spiritual connection is more pronounced than ever. Marcie has displayed remarkable resilience and consistency in her communication with God. She has cultivated a lifestyle of prayer that transcends mere religious practice, becoming a living testimony of the transformative power of a vibrant prayer life.

As you delve into the pages of "Pray and Pause", you will uncover a profound truth: prayer is not merely a one-way conversation, but a divine dialogue where God eagerly desires to share His wisdom and guidance with you. The "Pause" will reveal that there is a sacred exchange which extends beyond just your spoken words that will lead to revelation and communion.

This book is an indispensable resource. Prepare to be captivated, uplifted, and empowered as you embark on a transformative prayer expedition unlike any other. Allow the words to guide you on a journey of spiritual growth and intimacy with God, Embrace the invitation to enter a new space with God, knowing that in His presence, you will find the strength, wisdom, and grace to navigate life's challenges with confidence and peace. Let's not forget the FULLNESS of joy that is promised in the scripture. Get ready to embark on a soul-stirring pilgrimage of prayer that will reshape your spiritual landscape and deepen your walk with the One who eagerly awaits to commune with you.

Enjoy!

Portia Taylor

Pastor, VCMI Charles County

Author of the bestselling books, I'm Not That Woman and Audacity

"There is a place near me..."

> GOD SAID, LOOK,
> **HERE IS A PLACE RIGHT BESIDE ME.**
> *exodus 33:21*

"Father, thank You for this day. Thank You for Your presence in this very moment. I'm pausing to take it in... I don't ever want to forget Your promise to never leave or abandon me. (Deuteronomy 31:8; Hebrews 13:5) In Exodus You told Moses "Look, here is a place right beside me." When it all just seems to be "too much" and even when things are going well; thank You for Your gentle reminder that You've also reserved a place there for me... In Jesus' name. Amen."

Exodus 33 (NIV) begins with God telling Moses to "*Go...*" (vs.1) Him and the people He had just delivered up from the land of Egypt. He gave instructions to "*head for the land promised to Abraham, Isaac, and Jacob...*" He continued by promising him protection, provision, and His presence. The chapter concludes with God telling him "**There is a place near me***...*" (vs. 21). Friend, I came to tell you, there is a place near Him for you and me as well.

It was in my 'cleft' that this prayer devotional, and many others were conceived. In that place near Him, tears are cried, vision is birthed, my joy becomes full, intercession is plenty, and so much more. In that place near Him, I communicate with Him. At times He speaks through the Words of scripture etched in my heart, sometimes it's audible, or through confirmation, and at other times it's through a picture, an image, or still small voice. What's important is that I *pause* long enough afterward to hear His voice.

What happens after the pause is worth the wait.

At the time of my writing, the richest person in the world is Bernard Arnault. Arnault, whose current net worth is 210.1 billion, is the CEO and chairman at Moët Hennessy Louis Vuitton (LVMH), the world's largest luxury goods company comprising around 70 renowned fashion and cosmetics brands. Significant names in its portfolio include Louis Vuitton, Christian Dior, and Sephora (Forbesindia.com, 2024). If you were privileged to have an audience with Arnault to inquire about how he acquired his wealth, you'd most likely have no words, but rather sit quietly to hear what he had to say. However, *if* you were fortunate enough to have a one-on-one with him to ask questions, it's ludicrous to imagine you'd get up and walk away before he had the opportunity to respond. So why do we do that with God?

Prayer, simply put, is a conversation with God. The way He showed it to me – and I realize this is different for you – was He and I sitting down to have a conversation at a card table. I laid out my cards (my plan and my truth (Proverbs 14:12)), and He laid out His (His plan and His truth (Jeremiah 29:11)). Then He took my cards and gave me His. We stood up and He said, *"My Word won't return to me without doing what I send them to do."* (Isaiah 55:11 CEV)

The details of your day-to-day activity are all important to the "expected end" He has for your life.

Now first, for context, I was a bomb spades player back in the day. You didn't want to see me! LOL! And I know by saying that I might have just dated myself but stay with me... That's why the card table was relatable for me.

Second, that may not have landed with you, the way it did me. And that's okay. That was nearly 25 years ago but 'in that place near Him' my life was changed. Did it make everything "perfect" or instantly make me a better person? Did it cause me to never question God again, the way Moses did after countless times of meeting with Him face-to-face in the "tent of meeting" (vs. 7-11). No. My friend, it gave me the strength I needed to "press on to see what the end was gonna be" as my grandmother used to say. Because 'in a place near Him', I learned that The One who holds my future *saw me* when His glory passed by (vs. 22). *He sees you too...*

Our conversations with God were never supposed to be one-sided. There will be times that we talk, cry, and ask why and He listens. There will also be times that we sit silently in His presence. But we should never end the conversation without hearing His voice.

Pray & Pause is your invitation into a conversation. One where you *prime the prayer pump* as you enter His gates with thanksgiving and praise (Psalm 100:4 KJV). Tell God what you need and thank him for all He has done!" (Philippians 4:6 NLT). Take time to ask Him questions, empty your heart, or muse in silent prayer. And sit 'in a place near Him", allow His glory to pass, and hear from The One who would withhold no good thing from you (Psalms 84:11 KJV).

This prayer devotional was designed to provide you with "Prayer Starters" (the next volume in this series), conversation starters if you will, that were birthed from my personal time 'in a place near Him' early in the morning.

What is YOUR 'early?'

I know all our days, lives, and work schedules look different, but there is absolutely something to be said about seeking Him early in the morning. Mark 1:35 (AMP) tells us, "*In the early morning, while it was still dark, Jesus got up, left the house, and went away to a secluded place, and was praying there.*" Did you also know that George Washington Carver attributes his discovery of more than 300 uses of the peanut to wisdom God gave him, as he woke daily at 4:00 am to go into the woods and talk with God? Carver said:

> *"All my life, I have risen regularly at four in the morning
> to go into the woods and talk with God.
> That's where He reveals His secrets to me.
> When everybody else is asleep,
> I hear God best and learn my plan..."*

Whatever time you rise to have conversation with God, is between you and Him. What's important is that you have it. And more importantly, *'in that secluded place near Him'*, you learn THE plan.

Psalms 25:14-15 in The Passion Trasnlation tells us *"There's a private place reserved for the devoted lovers of YAHWEH, where they sit near him and receive the revelation-secrets of his promises."* That tells me that just like Moses, there is a place reserved near God, for me... and you.

Are you tired? Worn out? Burned out on religion?

Will you accept the invitation to journey through the following pages and *"Come to me. Get away with me and you'll recover your life. I'll show you how to take a real rest. Walk with me and work with me— watch how I do it. Learn the unforced rhythms of grace. I won't lay anything heavy or ill-fitting on you. Keep company with me and you'll learn to live freely and lightly."* (Matthew 11:28 MSG).

Each day starts a scripture image. Images created from pictures taken by some pretty amazing photographers (whose attributions can be found at the back of this prayer devotional), which I envisioned, as I meditated on each scripture. Next, is your Prayer Starter, laced with scripture, to ignite your time of prayer, followed by simple prompts to aid in your time of devotion. You are then invited to Pause and take time to capture what God has to show, impress upon, or speak to you.

So, are you ready to *Pray & Pause*? I can't begin to tell you how excited I am for what you're about to experience!

Marcie

Let the journey begin...

> BUT BLESSED IS THE ONE WHO TRUSTS IN THE LORD, WHOSE CONFIDENCE IS IN HIM. **THEY WILL BE LIKE** A TREE PLANTED BY THE WATER THAT SENDS OUT ITS ROOTS BY THE STREAM. IT DOES NOT FEAR WHEN HEAT COMES; ITS LEAVES ARE ALWAYS GREEN. IT HAS NO WORRIES IN A YEAR OF DROUGHT AND NEVER FAILS TO BEAR FRUIT.
>
> *Jeremiah 17:7-8*

Pray . . .

Father, I thank You for this day and these moments with You in Your Word. Word that reminds me that while at times my life may look dry and lifeless, I am blessed, and I will bloom again because my trust and confidence is in You! And like a tree planted by streams of living waters with deep roots that sustain me during the hardest of times, (Jeremiah 17:7-8) I am firmly planted in You. It is through You that I am able to live, to do what I do, and to be who I am (Acts 17:28). And all of this not just so I can survive and thrive in my own circumstances, but also so those around me can be blessed by my faith and turn to You. Thank You for being such a good Father and for providing for me in every area of my life (Genesis 22:14). You are unmatched (Psalm 113:5; Deuteronomy 33:26)! In Jesus' name, Amen.

What area do you need God to breathe life into right now?

Now Pause silently in His presence . . .

Close your eyes. . . What do you hear... feel... see...?

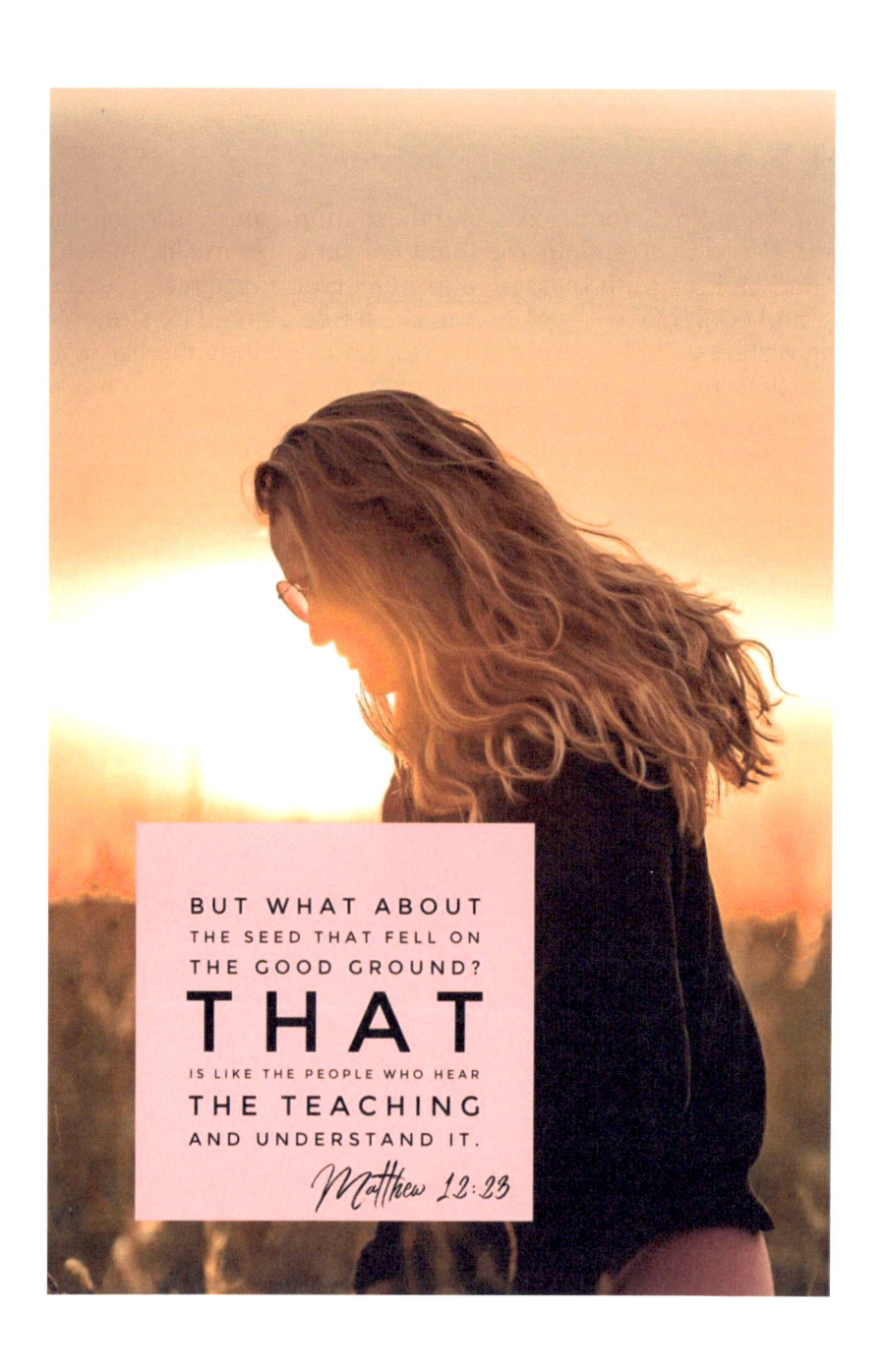

BUT WHAT ABOUT THE SEED THAT FELL ON THE GOOD GROUND? **THAT** IS LIKE THE PEOPLE WHO HEAR **THE TEACHING** AND UNDERSTAND IT.

Matthew 12:23

Pray...

Father, thank You for this day. Thank You for waking me this morning with a roof over my head and a bed to sleep in–things that many of us subconsciously take for granted. Father, as I prepare my heart, mind, and body for the day ahead, I look to You. I ask You to circumcise my heart to be sensitive to Your voice, the promptings of the Holy Spirit, and the needs of those around me. Show me opportunities to be Your hands and feet (Deuteronomy 10:12-22 ERV). I renew my mind by meditating on Your Word keeping my thoughts continually fixed on all that is authentic and real, honorable, and admirable, beautiful, and respectful, pure, and holy, merciful and kind (Philippians 4:8 TPT). Holy Spirit, help me to unlearn the parts of culture that do not profit me or bring You glory. Help me not to be conformed to this world but to rather be transformed by the daily (and sometimes moment by moment) renewing of my mind (Romans 12:2 ESV). Let my life represent that of a seed that falls on good ground. I want to be an example of one who hears the teaching and understands it, who grows and produces a good crop, sometimes 60 times more, and sometimes 30 times more (Matthew 13:23 ERV). I exercise my body, remembering that it is the temple of the Holy Spirit and that I am not my own (1 Corinthians 6:19). I discipline my body and keep it under control (1 Corinthians 9:27 ESV). As I and my family step through this day, Father I ask that You send Your angels to go before us, walk beside us, and to cover us from behind. Clothed in the armor of God (Ephesians 6:10-18), we can face whatever comes our way. In Jesus' name, Amen.

Now Pause silently in His presence...
Close your eyes... What do you hear... feel... see...?

ALL OF YOUR PRAYERS AND YOUR GENEROSITY TO THE POOR HAVE ASCENDED BEFORE GOD AS AN ETERNAL OFFERING.

acts 10:4

Pray...

Father, thank You. Thank You for Your love, grace, mercy, and forgiveness. Thank You for breath in my lungs and for Your promise of health and healing for my body. Thank You for my family and friends. Father, I pray that You would bless them and meet each one of them right where they are. Shower them with Your love. Be gracious to them and cover them with peace. As I continue through my day in tasks and in fervent prayer, I thank You Father that "all of my prayers and my generosity to those less fortunate have ascended before You as an eternal offering." (Acts 10:4) Thank You, Holy Spirit for guiding the steps of my day–ordering each one so that I accomplish what is necessary. In Jesus' name, Amen.

Who can you surprise with a note, text, call, gift, or token of appreciation today? Take a moment to write your own prayer for them here:

Now Pause silently in His presence...
Close your eyes... What do you hear... feel... see...?

HE WILL GUARD
AND GUIDE ME,
NEVER LETTING ME
STUMBLE OR FALL.
GOD IS MY KEEPER, HE WILL
NEVER FORGET
NOR IGNORE ME.

Psalms 121:3

Pray . . .

Father, I thank You for all the ways that You take care of me, look out for me, see my needs, and meet them. In Jesus' name, Amen.

List some of the ways God has provided for you:

Take a few minutes to Praise and Thank Him!

Now Pause silently in His presence . . .
Close your eyes. . . What do you hear... feel... see...?

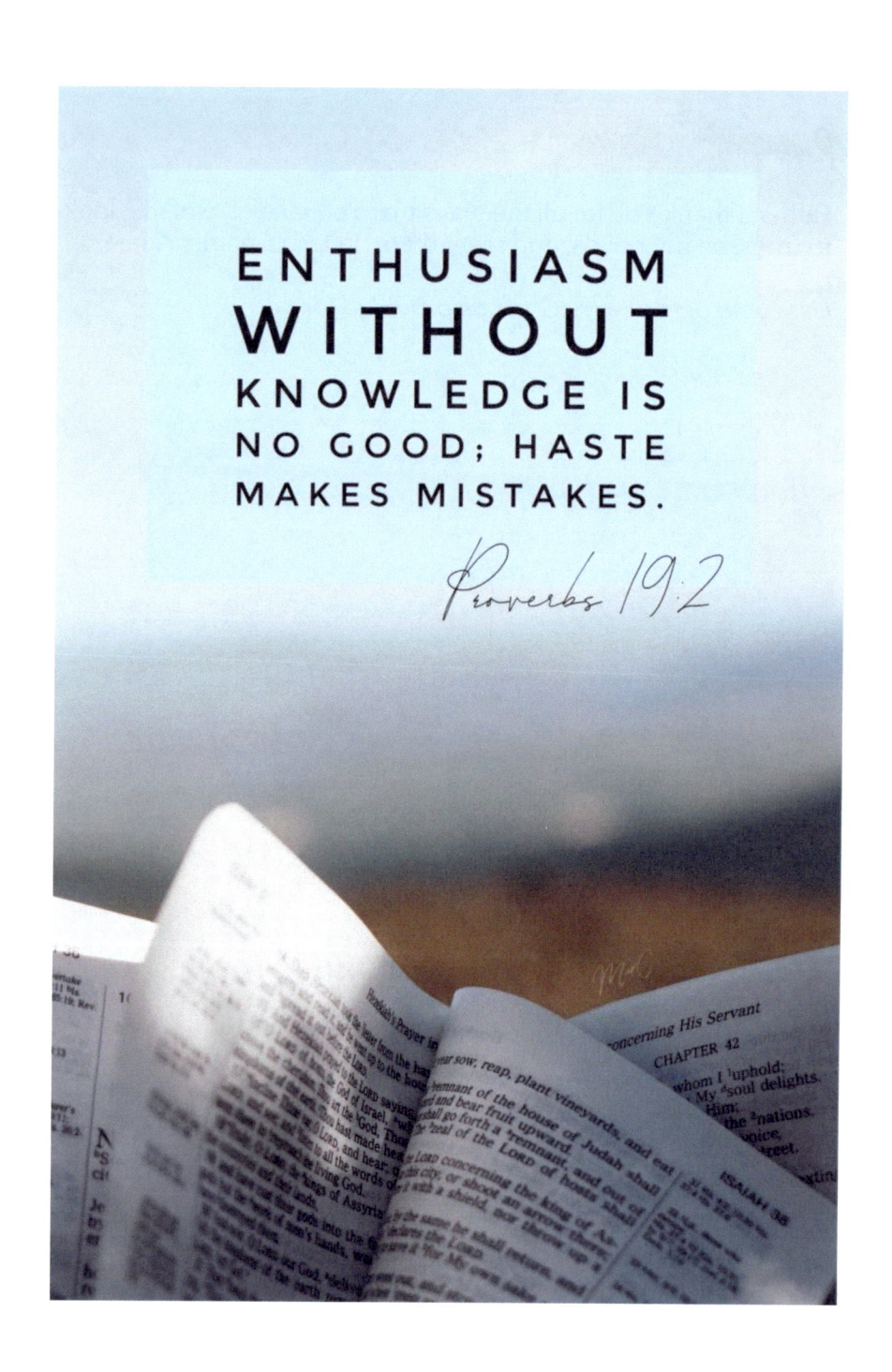

ENTHUSIASM **WITHOUT** KNOWLEDGE IS NO GOOD; HASTE MAKES MISTAKES.

Proverbs 19:2

Pray . . .

Father, thank You for this day. And thank You for creating rest. I am thankful for the fact that You never hurry, even when I may want You to rush. I thank You that Your timing is perfect and that in the waiting, You are cultivating the Fruit of Your Spirit in me, and I too am learning to take the time to give everything my best effort as I think them through. Keep me reminded of this as I go through my day and prepare for the days ahead. In Jesus' name. Amen.

What is a situation where you need to pump the brakes and pray? Take a moment to write that prayer to God and ask for His help:

Now Pause silently in His presence . . .
Close your eyes. . . What do you hear... feel... see....?

THANK GOD NO MATTER WHAT HAPPENS.

1 thessalonians 5:18

Pray . . .

Father, thank You for choosing to open my eyes today. I don't take that for granted. I make the decision to ALWAYS be joyful, NEVER stop praying, and in EVERYTHING I will give You thanks. (1 Thessalonians 5:16-18) In Jesus' name, Amen!

What are you thankful for at this moment? Father, I'm grateful! Let me count the ways...

1.

2.

3.

4.

5.

6.

7.

You don't have to stop there! Keep it going!

Now Pause silently in His presence . . .
Close your eyes. . . What do you hear... feel... see...?

WE ACKNOWLEDGE
YOU AS OUR
PROVIDER
OF ALL
WE NEED
EACH DAY.
MATTHEW 6:11

Pray...

Our Beloved Father dwelling in the heavenly realms, may the glory of Your name be the center on which our lives turn. Manifest Your kingdom realm, and cause Your every purpose to be fulfilled on earth, just as it is in heaven. We acknowledge You as our Provider of all we need each day. Forgive us the wrongs we have done as we ourselves release forgiveness to those who have wronged us. Rescue us every time we face tribulation and set us free from evil. For you are the King who rules with power and glory forever. Amen. (Matthew 6:9-13 TPT).

Sometimes we forget about the many ways God has provided for us. Take a moment to reflect on a time He's met a need and capture that memory here.

_____
_____
_____
_____
_____
_____
_____

In Isaiah 43:26, God says, "Put me in remembrance..." Surely, it's not because He's forgotten. He wants to make sure you remember what He said. Because if He did it before, He will do it again!

Now Pause silently in His presence...
Close your eyes... What do you hear... feel... see...?

_____
_____
_____
_____
_____

> ON THE SEVENTH DAY GOD HAD **FINISHED HIS WORK OF CREATION, SO HE** RESTED FROM ALL HIS WORK.
>
> *Genesis 2:2*

Pray . . .

Father, there's so much going on. In the world... In my mind... But I still thank You. The list of "to-do's" often seems endless. But then I pause like I am doing in this moment, and I'm reminded that just like You ordained work, You've ordained rest. Help me remember to set aside time to do that. To put down my phone. To close the laptop. To slow down, step away and maybe even take a nap. In the same way You rested from all Your work (Genesis 2:2), teach me how to do the same. In Jesus' name, Amen.

There are many ways that you can be proactive about taking the time to rest. A few are:

1. Ask Holy Spirit to nudge you (then be sure to listen).

2. Ask a trusted family member/friend to hold you accountable for taking time to rest and giving you a nudge. Who is that?
   _____

3. Add a recurring reminder to your phone to take 1 minute to pause and sit silently.

4. Add another recurring reminder to your phone to pause and practice deep breathing for 3 minutes. Let's practice now...

   Inhale through your nose for 1... 2... 3...
   Hold for 1... 2... 3...
   Breathe out of your mouth for 1... 2... 3...
   Repeat...

Now Pause silently in His presence . . .
Close your eyes. . . What do you hear... feel... see...?

_____
_____
_____
_____

> AND IF ANYONE LONGS TO BE WISE, **ASK** GOD FOR WISDOM AND HE WILL GIVE IT!
>
> JAMES 1:5

Pray...

Father, thank You for this day. And thank You for giving me clarity as I focus on my intentions for the day and weeks ahead. I've got multiple things to accomplish and conversations to have. Some will be almost effortless, while others will require wisdom because distractions will be many. You said that if I lack wisdom, I should ask You, who gives generously to all without finding fault, and it will be given to me (James 1:5) I'm careful to be mindful of that and to live each day with intentionality. And I know that I can do all things through Christ because He is my strength. (Philippians 4:13). Thank You, Father for ordering each of my steps. In Jesus' name, Amen.

In what current situation do you need God's wisdom? Tell Him about it here. Then open your heart to hear what He has to say.

Now Pause silently in His presence...
Close your eyes... What do you hear... feel... see...?

> WORK WILLINGLY AT WHATEVER YOU DO, AS THOUGH YOU WERE WORKING FOR THE LORD RATHER THAN FOR PEOPLE.
>
> *Colossians 3:23*

Pray . . .

Father, thank You for this day. I'm mindful in this moment of the work You have called me to do and the tasks I must perform daily to accomplish it. Many in our culture think hard work is a curse word. They say, "you should work smarter, not harder," but there's still something to be said for working hard. There's something satisfying about giving it your all! Everything won't be easy, and lasting results take effort. Wisdom is not given to replace work. Wisdom has taught me that work will at times require early mornings and late nights and may come with sweat and mental exhaustion. But that's only a bad thing if I forget the Sabbath (Exodus 20:8) *Selah*... Help me to remember that I should work willingly at whatever I do, as though I were working for You rather than for people (Colossians 3:23). That I am to use my hands for good hard work, and then give generously to others in need (Ephesians 4:28). Please help me to keep my eyes on the promise that I will enjoy the fruit of my labor (Proverbs 128:2), and that the sleep of those that labor is sweet (Ecclesiastes 5:12) *Selah*... Father, let me always be found to be an honest, hard worker, and a witness for Jesus, knowing that everything I do is ultimately for You. In Jesus' name. Amen.

What work has God called YOU to do, that you – like Nehemiah (Nehemiah 6:3) – can't come down from? What's one step you can take towards that today?

Now Pause silently in His presence . . .
Close your eyes. . . What do you hear... feel... see...?

> LET THE WISE LISTEN AND ADD TO THEIR **LEARNING,** AND LET THE DISCERNING GET GUIDANCE—
>
> *Proverbs 1:5*

Pray . . .

Father, thank You for this day and time in Your Word. It reminds me that "the wise hear and increase in learning and those with understanding attain wise counsel" (Proverbs 1:5), Father, let me be found wise and discerning. I ask You to fill me with wisdom for every decision I need to make today and, in the days, ahead. Cause me to hear the truth and know it. Father, I ask that You give me wisdom in all I do so my life will be shaped by Your hands and not the world. In Jesus' name, Amen.

In what area have you been relying on your own wisdom? Making decisions without consulting God. Be specific. Write it down here:

Using the SOAP method, write out and think on Proverbs 1:5

S – Write the **Scripture**:

O – What do you **OBSERVE**?

A – How can you **APPLY** it to your life?

P – Now **PRAY** about it ...

Now Pause silently in His presence . . .
Close your eyes. . . What do you hear... feel... see...?

IN EVERYTHING,
GIVE THANKS.

1 THESSALONIANS 5:18

Pray . . .

Father, I just want to pause and say, Thank You!

If you had ten thousand tongues, it would not be enough to thank Him for who He is, all He's done, and has yet to do. But since you have these few lines, give it a go. You'll no doubt run out of room!

Now Pause silently in His presence . . .
Close your eyes. . . What do you hear... feel... see...?

> IN EVERYTHING YOU DO, PUT GOD FIRST, AND HE WILL DIRECT YOU AND CROWN YOUR EFFORTS WITH SUCCESS.
>
> PSALM 3:6

Pray . . .

Father, thank You for this day. I'll soon be off and running with the things I hope to accomplish, but not before pausing in Your presence. Your Word reminds me that if I put You first in everything I do, You will direct me and crown my efforts with success (Proverbs 3:6). Father, I give You thanks and praise, and I keep You first in my heart and in every area of my life. Thank You for guiding my footsteps and the work I put my hands to today. Thank You for every favorable outcome. And more than that, thank You for being with me every step of the way. In Jesus' name, Amen.

In what area have you not put God first? Take a moment to repent and ask God to crown your efforts:

Now Pause silently in His presence . . .
Close your eyes. . . What do you hear... feel... see...?

IT TAKES MORE THAN BREAD TO STAY ALIVE. IT TAKES A STEADY STREAM OF WORDS FROM GOD'S MOUTH.

matthew 4:4

Pray . . .

Father, thank You for this day. Starting and ending my day with time in Your presence and Word is vital to my life because I don't live by food alone—I need a steady stream of Words from Your mouth (Matthew 4:4). Holy Spirit, keep me reminded of this as I move throughout my days. It's the only way I can make the best decisions in every circumstance so my progress will continue to be limitless as I continue to walk with You (Proverbs 4:12). In Jesus' name. Amen.

What Words (scriptures) are you feeding on today? Make note of them here, then take a moment to meditate on them, hiding them in your heart (Psalm 119:11):

Now Pause silently in His presence . . .
Close your eyes. . . What do you hear... feel... see...?

LOOK WITH WONDER AT THE DEPTH OF THE FATHER'S MARVELOUS LOVE THAT HE HAS LAVISHED ON US! HE HAS CALLED US AND MADE US HIS VERY OWN BELOVED CHILDREN...

1 John 3:1

Pray . . .

Father, I thank You for this day. I thank You for the family and friends You've given me to do life with. I thank You for the space they hold in my life, and the value we add to one another. And while I wouldn't trade my village for another, I marvel in this moment at the privilege to be in a relationship with You. To be called Your own. An adult with responsibilities of my own, but still Your child (1 John 3:1). Father, nothing in this world could ever take Your place. And I Thank You for taking such good care of me. You are so much better than anything I ever wanted or thought I needed. In Jesus' name. Amen.

Which family members or friends come to mind right now? List their names below and lift them in prayer throughout the day:

_____
_____
_____
_____
_____
_____
_____
_____
_____
_____
_____
_____
_____

Now Pause silently in His presence . . .
Close your eyes. . . What do you hear... feel... see...?

_____
_____
_____
_____

Clothe yourself with

COMPASSION
KINDNESS HUMILITY
GENTLENESS PATIENCE

Colossians 3:12

Pray . . .

Father, thank You for this day. And thank You for the truth and direction I can always find in Your Word. I'm reminded today that what I possess internally in Christ is what really matters. So, as I choose what I'll outwardly wear for these meetings, errands, and such, I first pause to clothe myself with compassion, kindness, humility, gentleness, and patience. Holy Spirit, I ask You to help me to be merciful as I endeavor to understand others, and to be compassionate, showing kindness toward all. Remind me to be gentle and humble, unoffendable in my patience with others (Colossians 3:12). These are the 'garments' that matter most as I represent You. In Jesus' name. Amen.

What are you "wearing" today? Is it compassion, kindness, or empathy? If it is, ask God to increase it. If it's not, pause for a moment and write a note asking God to redress you:

Now Pause silently in His presence . . .
Close your eyes. . . What do you hear... feel... see...?

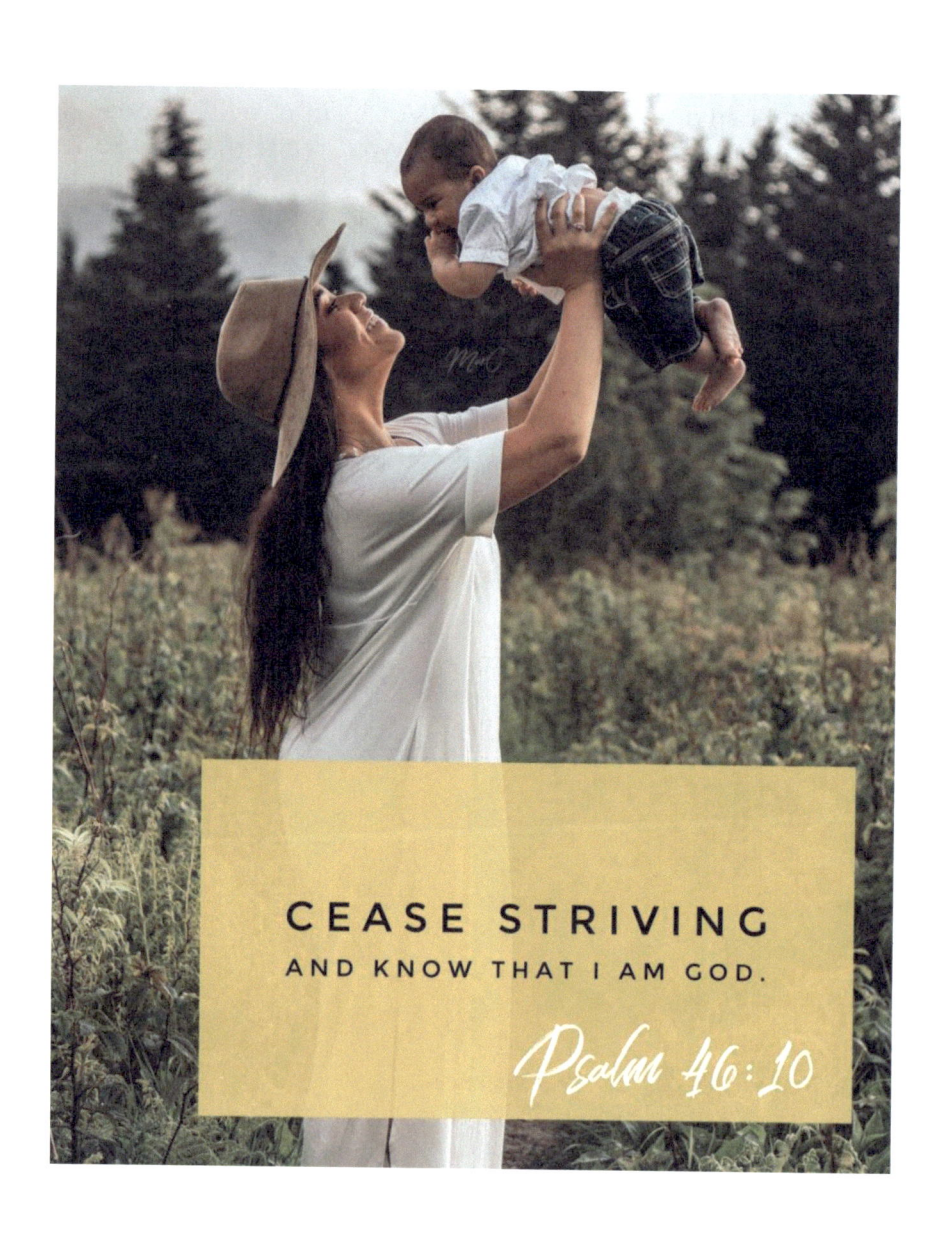

CEASE STRIVING
AND KNOW THAT I AM GOD.

Psalm 46:10

Pray . . .

Father, You desire for us to trust You first in all we do. Not after we've created our vision boards and have written out our to-do lists, but first. I admit that I've been guilty of this some days. And right now, I pause to repent. Every day—yes, even Saturdays and Sundays—is Yours. If I'm honest, sometimes I think the weekends belong to me. Father, I will cease striving and rest in knowing that You are God (Psalm 46:10a). It is senseless to work hard from early morning till late at night, toiling to make a living for fear of not having enough when You can provide for me even while I sleep. Unless You build my house, I labor in vain (Psalm 127:2). *Selah...* Father, redirect my focus today. Set me on the right path. Give me an entirely different approach to thinking about time. Help me to understand Your goals for my time and to put trust in You at the center of how I use it. Father, show me how to spend my days. When to rise, when to lay my head to sleep, and everything in between. In Jesus' name. Amen.

What is the most important area that needs your focus today?

Now Pause silently in His presence . . .

Close your eyes. . . What do you hear... feel... see...?

SET YOUR GAZE ON THE PATH BEFORE YOU. WITH FIXED **PURPOSE, LOOKING** STRAIGHT AHEAD, IGNORE LIFE'S **DISTRACTIONS.**

PROVERBS 4:25

Pray . . .

Father, thank You for this day. I'm pausing in Your presence and Your Word to renew my mind (Romans 12:2), set my priorities, and prepare for the day. Father, I "set my gaze on the path before me. With fixed purpose, looking straight ahead, ignoring life's distractions (Proverbs 4:25). I'm asking You to open my eyes to the distractions that keep sidelining my priorities. The calls/texts, event invitations, social media scrolling, and more that seem harmless, but often divert me from intentional living. Holy Spirit help me to remain focused and disciplined to keep the most important things first. In Jesus' name. Amen.

What are your top 5 priorities today? List them here and ask Holy Spirit to help keep you focused on them:

1.

2.

3.

4.

5.

Now Pause silently in His presence . . .

Close your eyes. . . What do you hear... feel... see...?

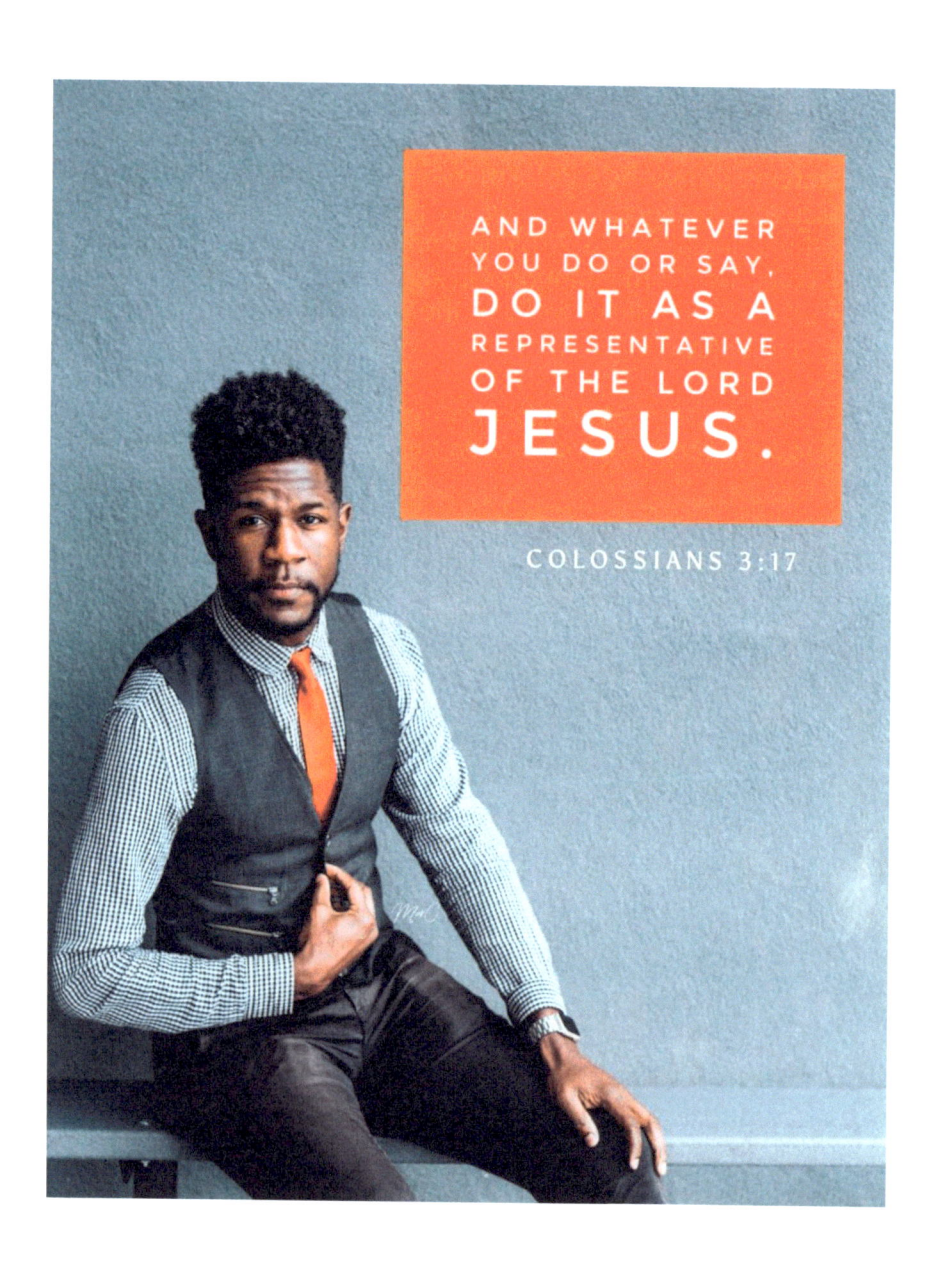

AND WHATEVER YOU DO OR SAY, **DO IT AS A** REPRESENTATIVE OF THE LORD **JESUS.**

COLOSSIANS 3:17

Pray...

Father, thank You for this day. Thank You for Your Word that gives direction and brings correction to my life. Father my desire is to live my life not only in Your great grace and mercies, but with conviction to the gospel. Not being afraid of criticism, but always following the truth of Your Word, even when it's not popular. It's more important to me to be right with You than with people. And with the help of Holy Spirit, in whatever I do or say, I'll do it as a representative of the Lord Jesus (Colossians 3:17). In His name I pray, Amen.

Take a moment to speak over your day! Write a declaration of what it will be:

Now Pause silently in His presence...

Close your eyes... What do you hear... feel... see...?

THIS IS MY COMMAND—BE **STRONG AND COURAGEOUS!** DO NOT BE AFRAID OR DISCOURAGED. FOR THE LORD YOUR GOD IS **WITH YOU** WHEREVER YOU GO.

JOSHUA 1:9

Pray . . .

Father, I thank You for this day. And I thank You for Your goodness and grace. Time in Your Word reminds me that You don't give me hard things and then leave me to fend for myself. Like You did with Esther, Joshua, and countless others, You promised to walk with and equip me for any and everything. I receive Your command to be strong and courageous today (Joshua 1:9). I thank You for blessing everything I put my hands to (Deuteronomy 28:8). I thank You for making my progress limitless and for creating a clear and open path before me (Proverbs 4:12)! In Jesus' name, Amen.

Where do you need to be courageous today? Ask God to give you the strategy you need. Pause and listen for it and write what you hear:

Now Pause silently in His presence . . .
Close your eyes. . . What do you hear... feel... see...?

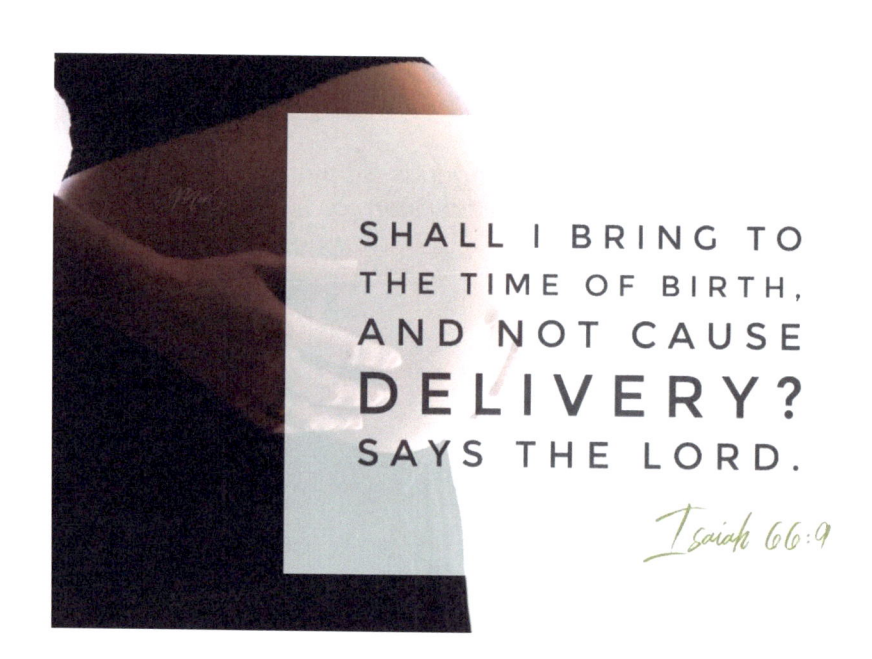

SHALL I BRING TO THE TIME OF BIRTH, AND NOT CAUSE DELIVERY? SAYS THE LORD.

Isaiah 66:9

Pray...

Father, thank You for this day. Time with You reminds me and reveals to me what You are doing in and through me. I recognize that You are taking me to a new place of faith and maturity, and that You're using everything I'm going through to develop something new in me. I feel the birthing pains of my purpose being delivered, and it hurts! Labor is neither clean nor pretty, but I take heart knowing that You are THE deliverer! You would not bring me to the time of birth and not cause delivery (Isaiah 66:9). Success is imminent! Father, I'll do my part. I'LL KEEP PUSHING! I trust You to handle the rest. All of it. In Jesus' name. Amen.

What "new" do you sense God is birthing in you? Write it here and PUUUUUUUUSH!!!

Now Pause silently in His presence...
Close your eyes... What do you hear... feel... see...?

> WHAT GOOD IS IT, DEAR BROTHERS AND SISTERS, IF YOU SAY YOU HAVE FAITH BUT DON'T SHOW IT BY YOUR ACTIONS?
>
> *james* 2:14

Pray...

Father, thank You for this day. Thank You for Your consistent grace and mercies. Time with You and Your Word both reminds and urges me to exercise my faith today. Because what good is it if I say I have faith but don't show it by my actions (James 2:14)? I believe the promises in Your Word and the things You've spoken to my heart in prayer. Today, I will do my part to make my faith come alive! To allow it to transform from what I believe internally to what I do externally. Showing my faith, by my good deeds (James 2:18). In Jesus' name. Amen

Where do you need to exercise your faith today? Since faith is an action word – "...faith apart from works is useless." (James 2:20b) – what action will you take today?

Now Pause silently in His presence...
Close your eyes... What do you hear... feel... see...?

> GOD IS WITHIN HER, SHE WILL **NOT FALL**; GOD WILL HELP HER AT BREAK OF DAY.
>
> PSALM 46:5

Pray...

Father, thank You for this day. I'm diving into the day with a heart and plan of intentions. I've set my heart first to please You in all I do—taking my everyday life and laying it before You as an offering (Romans 12:1). No, I won't forget that. Armed with strategies and full of thanksgiving that I have Holy Spirit as my guide, I'm walking into this day confidently. Head held high—no more shrinking back—ready to put in the work necessary (my part) to accomplish all I put my hands to. I know full well that because You are within me, I will not fall. I won't be moved, and I know You will help and protect me (Psalm 46:5). Thank You, Father. In Jesus' name. Amen

Where specifically do you need God's help or wisdom? What is your part? What step will you take today?

Now Pause silently in His presence...

Close your eyes... What do you hear... feel... see...?

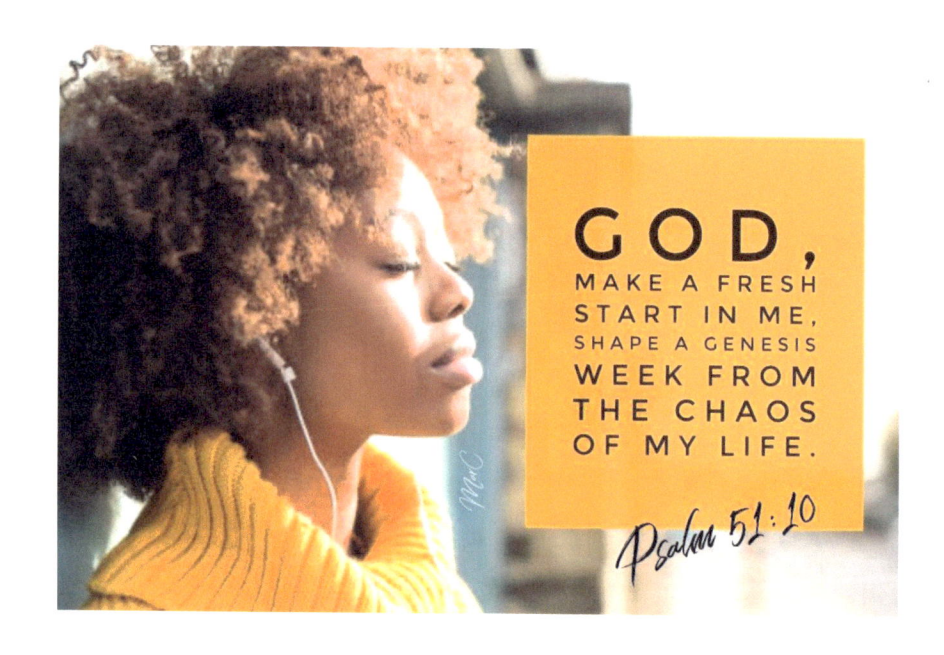

GOD, MAKE A FRESH START IN ME, SHAPE A GENESIS WEEK FROM THE CHAOS OF MY LIFE.

Psalm 51:10

Pray . . .

Father, I thank You. As I prepare for the days ahead, I'm pausing to spend intentional time in your presence. I ask You to make a fresh start in me (Psalm 51:10). Don't allow me to get lost in "resolutions" and "words." While both are good and have their place, I don't want to miss hearing the very specific things You saw when You pondered the thoughts and plans You have for me (Jeremiah 29:11). I'm pressing on to take hold of that for which Christ Jesus took hold of me and the purposes for which I was created (Philippians 3:12). Father, stir Your spirit within me and cause me to walk in Your statutes, and I will keep Your judgments and do them (Ezekiel 36:27). I can't lose focus of the needful things, so please help me Holy Spirit to remain focused. Guide my heart, my thoughts, and my steps. In Jesus' name. Amen.

What steps do you need to take to prepare for what you're believing God for? Start with three:

Step 1.

Step 2.

Step 3.

Now Pause silently in His presence . . .
Close your eyes. . . What do you hear... feel... see...?

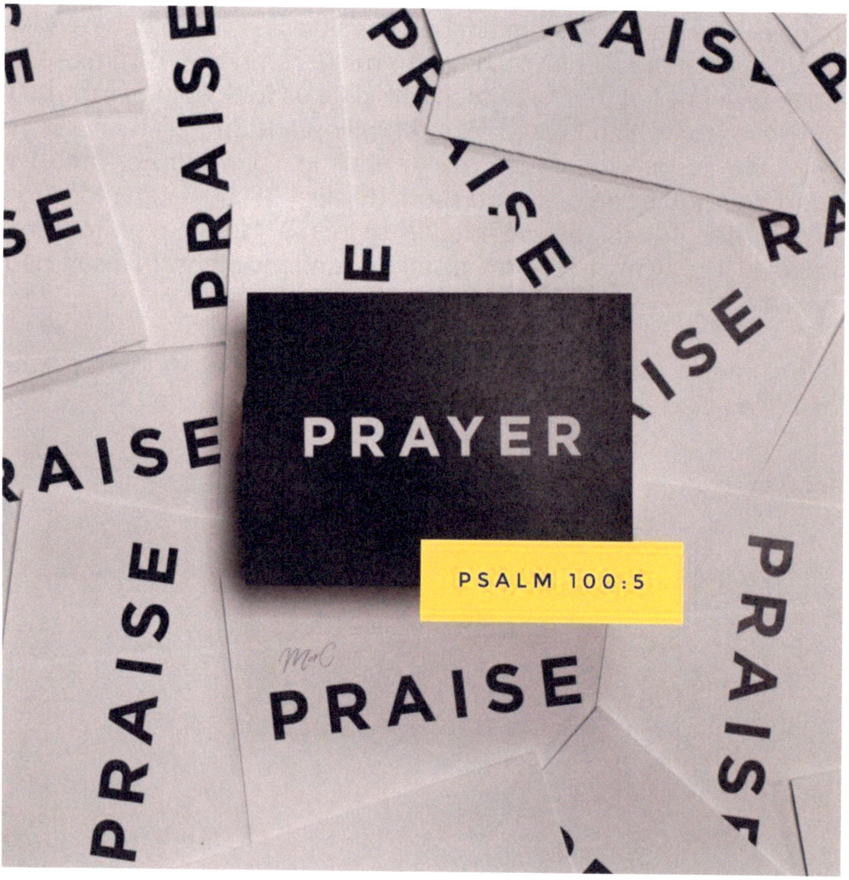
PRAISE
PRAISE
PRAYER
PSALM 100:5
PRAISE
PRAISE

Pray . . .

Father, You are Good! Your love never fails, and Your mercy lasts forever. I receive Your promise of faithfulness for me, my family and every one of Your children (Psalm 100:5). In Jesus' name. Amen.

What has God promised you? If you can't recall, pause and search the scripture (your Bible, the Bible app, or Google) and find a promise for what you're believing for. Write it here:

Scripture:
_____
_____
_____
_____

What stood out to you?
_____
_____
_____
_____

How will you apply it to your life?
_____
_____
_____
_____

Now Pause silently in His presence . . .
Close your eyes. . . What do you hear... feel... see...?

> IN THE MORNING, LORD, YOU HEAR MY VOICE; IN THE MORNING I LAY MY REQUESTS BEFORE YOU AND WAIT EXPECTANTLY.
>
> psalm 5:3

Pray...

Father, thank You for opening my eyes this morning. I'm reminded that when Your presence and Your Word are the first things I give my heart and mind to each day, I see (with the eyes of my heart) everything as under the control of my all-good, all-powerful, and all-loving heavenly Father. No matter how I feel (good or bad) or what things look like, You are GOOD and cause EVERYTHING to work together for my good because I love You. And for that, I thank You. In Jesus' name. Amen.

Starting your day in His presence and with His Word, is an intention of the heart. In what ways can you modify your evening and morning routine to start your day sharing your heart with the Father, and listening for what's on His? Ask Holy Spirit to show you:

Now Pause silently in His presence...
Close your eyes... What do you hear... feel... see...?

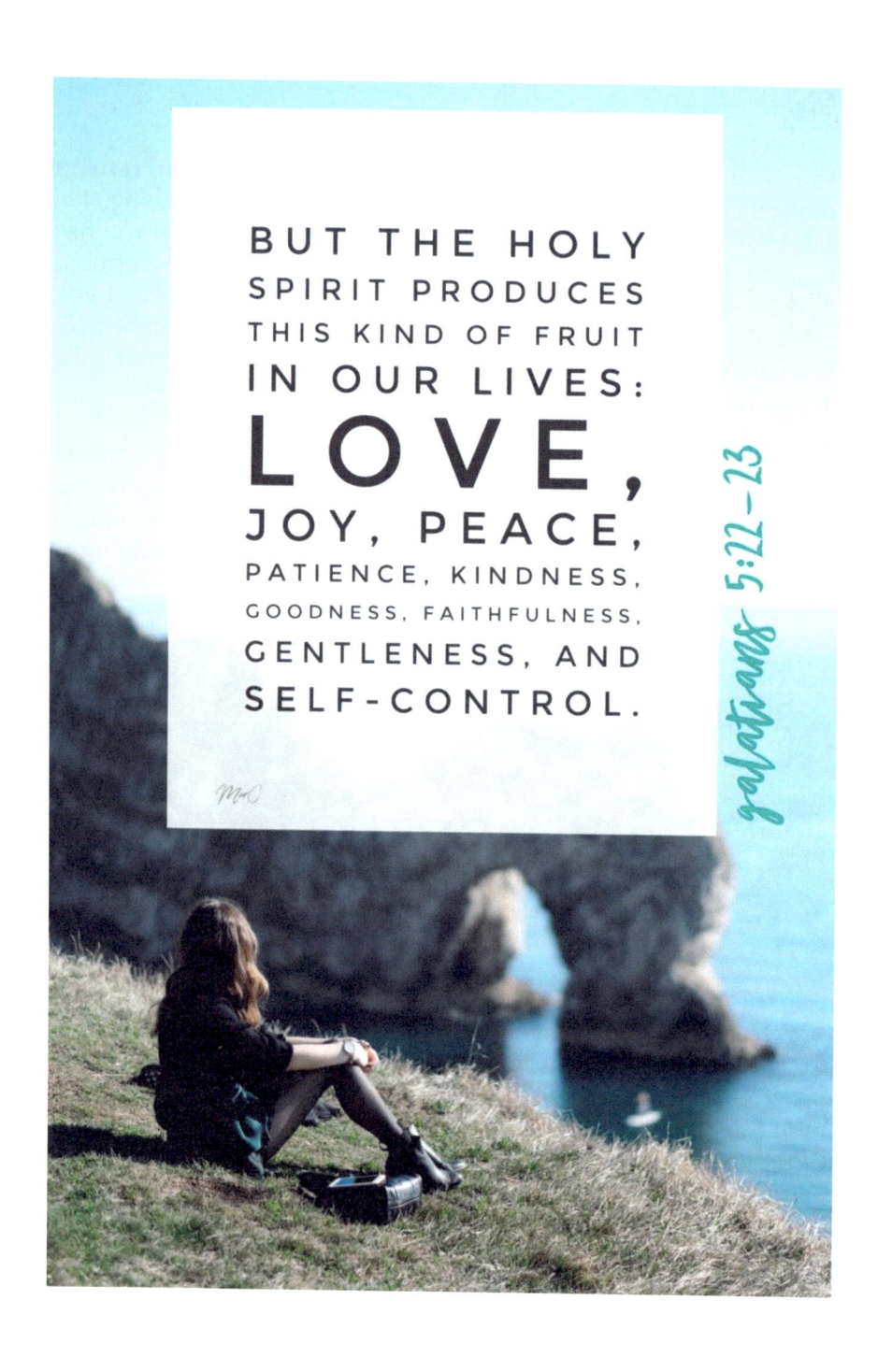

BUT THE HOLY SPIRIT PRODUCES THIS KIND OF FRUIT IN OUR LIVES: **LOVE, JOY, PEACE,** PATIENCE, KINDNESS, GOODNESS, FAITHFULNESS, GENTLENESS, AND SELF-CONTROL.

galatians 5:22–23

Pray . . .

Father, thank You for this day. And thank You for Your grace, mercy, and direction as I step through it. Holy Spirit, produce in me love, joy, peace, patience, kindness, goodness, faithfulness, gentleness, and self-control. I need Your help to accomplish this, and I yield to you. Father, in every task and interaction, I want to be a reflection of You. In Jesus' name. Amen.

Take a few moments to ponder on elements of the Fruit of the Spirit. After a moment with each one, circle it as an act of acceptance:

Love Joy Patience *Peace* *Kindness* Goodness **Self-Control** Faithfulness

Now Pause silently in His presence . . .
Close your eyes. . . What do you hear... feel... see...?

DON'T WORRY ABOUT ANYTHING; INSTEAD, PRAY ABOUT EVERYTHING. **TELL GOD WHAT YOU NEED,** AND THANK HIM FOR ALL HE HAS DONE.

Philippians 4:6-7

Pray . . .

Father, thank You for this day. And thank You for these moments with You. Thank You for the gentle reminder that prayer is not something I have to do. It's something that I *get* to do. I get to meet with the King of Kings... What a privilege! I'm thankful that I get to spend time with You before I dive into my day and as I walk through it. This shift in my perspective changes everything. It opens my eyes and heart to all the other things I *get* to do. Like, I *get* to do all things through Christ who gives me strength and I don't have to bear the burdens or face any task on my own. I *get* to recognize You at work in all my ways, so I don't have to lean on my own understanding (Proverbs 3:5-6). I *get* to pray about everything, instead of worrying about anything—telling You what I need and thanking You for what You've already done (Philippians 4:6-7). Father, You are so good to me... *Selah*... and I'm thankful to be called Your own. I need Your Holy Spirit every moment of every day to lead and guide me in all the things I *get* to do. In Jesus' name. Amen.

*What are you thankful that you **get** to do today? Start here by telling God what you need and thank Him for ALL He's done:*

Now Pause silently in His presence . . .
Close your eyes. . . What do you hear... feel... see...?

MY PRAYER
REACHED HIS EARS.

2 SAMUEL 22:7

Pray . . .

Father, I thank You. I thank You for Your grace, mercy, and kindness. And I'm so grateful that every time I call to You—whether in words or by silent tears—You hear me from Heaven and my prayer reaches Your ears (2 Samuel 22:7). Thank You for being with me in the most amazing as well as hardest moments of my life. You promised You'd never leave me or loose Your grip on my life (Hebrews 13:5). You're true to Your Word and for that I thank You. As I begin the tasks of my day, I won't forget how much I need You. In everything, big or small, I need Your guidance and I ask Your protection. Shed light on my path and everything I need to put my hands to. And Father, I ask for Your wisdom and protection from the things (people and wrong opportunities) that try to steal me away from my purpose. I'm ready for this day... Holy Spirit, lead the way. In Jesus' name. Amen.

In your own words, empty your heart to God here:

Now Pause silently in His presence . . .
Close your eyes. . . What do you hear... feel... see...?

TODAY,
WHILE THERE IS
STILL
OPPORTUNITY,
IF YOU HEAR
HIS VOICE,
DON'T DESENSITIZE
YOUR HEART.
hebrews 3:15
listen

Pray...

Father, thank You for this day, and thank You for the advice of Your Word. Thank you for your counsel to not become comfortable with where I am and your encouragement to keep pressing whenever I am faced with challenges (Philippians 3:14). Hebrews 3:15 reminds me today [while there is still opportunity] that if I hear Your voice, not to harden (or desensitize) my heart. Selah... I'm listening, Father. Help me to never become less sympathetic to the state of my family, community, and the world. I'm pausing to intentionally recall the direction from Your Word and those You spoke to my heart. With the Great Commission as my marching orders, I'll take every opportunity to teach those that I meet how You want us to live. I'll never forget that You are with me every moment of every day (Matthew 28:15-20). In Jesus' name. Amen.

What has God spoken to your heart? What are the specific instructions? If you have trouble hearing, find a scripture that speaks to the purpose in your heart. Write it here:

Now Pause silently in His presence...
Close your eyes... What do you hear... feel... see...?

Practice the Pause...

The pages that follow are an invitation for you to pause and write your own prayers. Begin by finding a scripture. Not sure where to look? Do a word search on something that's in your heart. Psalms is also a great place to start. David knew something about conversations with God!

Next, write the scripture at the top of the page. Why write it, you ask? Writing by hand forces your brain to process information in a more detailed way, which helps you successfully load that information into your memory. Another way to "hide the Word in your heart" (Psalms 19:11).

Finally, take a few minutes to meditate on the scripture. In other words, read it over a few times. Word by word... Speak it out loud. Then write the words that flood your heart.

Ready? Give it a go!

My Scripture:

My Prayer:

Now Pause silently in His presence . . .
Close your eyes. . . What do you hear... feel... see...?

My Scripture:

My Prayer:

Now Pause silently in His presence . . .
Close your eyes. . . What do you hear... feel... see...?

My Scripture:

My Prayer:

Now Pause silently in His presence . . .
Close your eyes. . . What do you hear... feel... see...?

My Scripture:

My Prayer:

Now Pause silently in His presence . . .
Close your eyes. . . What do you hear... feel... see...?

My Scripture:

My Prayer:

Now Pause silently in His presence . . .
Close your eyes. . . What do you hear... feel... see...?

My Scripture:

My Prayer:

Now Pause silently in His presence . . .
Close your eyes. . . What do you hear... feel... see...?

My Scripture:

My Prayer:

Now Pause silently in His presence . . .
Close your eyes. . . What do you hear... feel... see...?

My Scripture:

My Prayer:

Now Pause silently in His presence . . .
Close your eyes. . . What do you hear... feel... see...?

My Scripture:

My Prayer:

Now Pause silently in His presence . . .
Close your eyes. . . What do you hear... feel... see...?

My Scripture:

My Prayer:

Now Pause silently in His presence . . .
Close your eyes. . . What do you hear... feel... see...?

My Scripture:

My Prayer:

Now Pause silently in His presence . . .
Close your eyes. . . What do you hear... feel... see...?

My Scripture:

My Prayer:

Now Pause silently in His presence . . .
Close your eyes. . . What do you hear... feel... see...?

My Scripture:

My Prayer:

Now Pause silently in His presence . . .
Close your eyes. . . What do you hear... feel... see...?

Photo Attributions

Shoutout to all the amazing photographers on Unsplash.com who inspired the visual foundation for each prayer, before adding additional scriptures, elements, and in some cases, filters.

Page 7: Photographer unknown on Unsplash
Page 12: Photographer unknown on Unsplash
Page 14: Photo by Wasa Crispbread on Unsplash
Page 16: Photo by Allef Vinicius on Unsplash
Page 18: Photo by Jessica Delp on Unsplash
Page 20: Photo by Emmanuel Akinte on Unsplash
Page 22: Photo by Raychan on Unsplash
Page 24: Photo by Matteo Vistocco on Unsplash
Page 26: Photo by Collins Lesulie on Unsplash
Page 28: Photo by Simon Abrams on Unsplash
Page 30: Photo by Severin Höin on Unsplash
Page 32: Photo by Jon Tyson on Unsplash
Page 34: Photo by Severin Höin on Unsplash
Page 36: Photo by Gift Habeshaw on Unsplash
Page 38: Photo by Sean Kong on Unsplash
Page 40: Photo by Austin Wade on Unsplash
Page 42: Photo by Austin Wade on Unsplash
Page 44: Photo by Brooke Cagle on Unsplash
Page 46: Photo by Tyler Nix on Unsplash
Page 48: Photo by Sai De Silva on Unsplash
Page 50: Photo by freestocks on Unsplash
Page 52: Photo by Leonardo Zorzi on Unsplash
Page 54: Photo by Jasmin Chew on Unsplash
Page 56: Photographer unknown on Unsplash
Page 58: Photo by Yanin Diaz on Unsplash
Page 60: Photo by Guilherme Stecanella on Unsplash
Page 62: Photo by Robert Bye on Unsplash
Page 64: Photo by Kayle Kaupanger on Unsplash
Page 66: Photo by Julius Espiritu on Unsplash
Page 68: Photo by Adrian Hernandez on Unsplash

Typically, after my time of devotion and prayer then meditating on the scripture, I imagined what image could visually express what I saw. Unsplash.com was usually my go to, and the images always inspired my scripture images. Never thinking I'd turn these into a book, I didn't always capture the names of the amazingly gifted photographers. If you find the names of any missing, please reach out to me and share so I can attribute the appropriate credit. And if you ever need to be inspired, hop over to Unsplash.com and browse the fantastic gallery.

Enjoy, and support creatives!

Made in the USA
Columbia, SC
03 October 2024